W9-BOO-532

Forensic Crime Solvers

Computer Evidence

by Michael Dahl

Consultant:
Gary Amos
Certified Forensic Computer Examiner
President, Cyberlab Computer Forensics, LLC
Virginia Beach, Virginia

Capstone *press*

Mankato, Minnesota

Edge Books are published by Capstone Press
151 Good Counsel Drive, P.O. Box 669, Mankato, Minnesota 56002
www.capstonepress.com

Library of Congress Cataloging-in-Publication Data
Dahl, Michael.
    Computer evidence / by Michael Dahl.
    p. cm.—(Edge books. Forensic crime solvers)
    Includes bibliographical references and index.
    Contents: Threatening mail—Types of computer crime—Searching for evidence—
Fighting computer crime.
    ISBN 0-7368-2698-X (hardcover)
    1. Computer crimes—Investigation—Juvenile literature. [1. Computer crimes—
Investigation.] I. Title. II. Series.
HV8079.C65D34 2005
363.25'968—dc22   2003027978

Editorial Credits
Carrie A. Braulick, editor; Juliette Peters, series designer; Enoch Peterson, book
    designer; Jo Miller, photo researcher; Eric Kudalis, product planning editor

Photo Credits
AP Wide World Photos/Ann Heisenfelt, 15; Toby Talbot, 26
Bruce Coleman Inc./Leif Linder, 23; Norman Owen Tomalin, 1
Capstone Press/Gary Sundermeyer, 4, 6, 7, 8, 9
Corbis/John Madere, 10; Reuters NewMedia Inc., front cover, 12, 27
Corbis Sygma/J. T. Atlan, 14
Getty Images Inc./AFP/Kai-Uwe Knoth, 28; Joe Raedle, 24; Newsmakers/Alex Wong,
    16
Ingram Publishing, back cover
Mikael Karlsson, 18, 20

1 2 3 4 5 6 09 08 07 06 05 04

Table of Contents

CHAPTER 1

Learn about:

- A computer crime
- Search warrants
- Examining a computer

Threatening Mail

For the second week in a row, all the stores along Center Street received threats. Each morning, more threatening letters were in each store's mailbox. Some store owners also received e-mail threats. The letters and e-mails always said the same thing. The store owners were told to close their stores and leave Center Street. If they didn't leave, their stores would be destroyed.

The FBI Gets Involved

The local police had few clues to help them find the person who sent the threats. The letters were printed from a common computer printer. They were on plain white paper. Police found only the store owners' fingerprints on the letters and envelopes. The police asked local FBI agents for help.

Some store owners on Center
◀ Street received e-mail threats.

Tracing E-mail

The FBI agents tracked the threatening e-mails. One of the store owners had received threats from a sender called BuzzOff.net. The agents discovered that the name was registered with an Internet provider called Local Express.

Managers at Local Express gave the agents the name and address of the person using BuzzOff.net. The name and address belonged to a woman who lived in another state. The woman's name and credit card number had been stolen. The woman did not know about the threats.

A Suspect and a Search Warrant

FBI agents talked to each of the store owners. Many of the store owners talked about Ray Russell. Russell had applied for jobs at many

Investigators talked with each store owner about the threats.

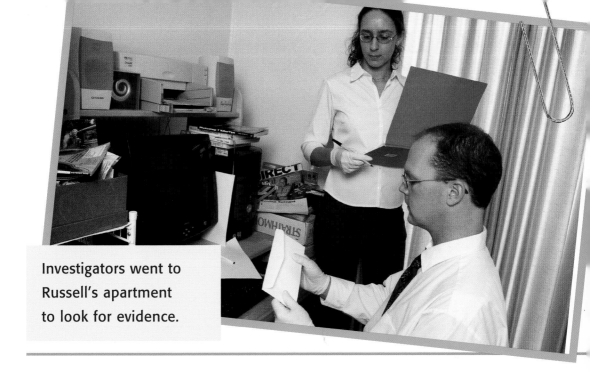

Investigators went to Russell's apartment to look for evidence.

of the stores. None of the stores offered him a job. The agents learned Russell had been arrested before for threatening others.

The FBI agents wanted to examine Russell's computer for evidence. They asked a judge for a search warrant. The judge gave them the warrant.

Seizing Russell's Computer

The FBI agents and two police officers went to Russell's apartment building. Russell was not there. The apartment building's manager unlocked Russell's door for them. The team entered the apartment. One police officer brought a video camera. He recorded the team's activities.

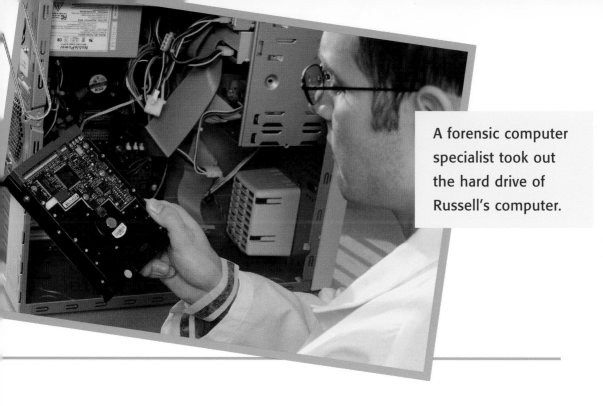

A forensic computer specialist took out the hard drive of Russell's computer.

One of the FBI agents carried a laptop computer. It had programs to peek at the documents in other computers. The agent found a list of folders and documents on Russell's computer. The folders were named for each of the Center Street stores. The computer also contained information about building bombs. This information gave the FBI agents a reason to take Russell's computer.

The agents put on latex gloves before handling the computer. They placed the computer in several large paper bags. They carried it out of Russell's apartment.

Examining the Computer

In the FBI computer lab, a forensic computer specialist took apart Russell's computer. He made copies of the hard drive. He then searched the copies for evidence.

The specialist found a document with two sentences typed at the top. The sentences had wording similar to the threatening letters. The document also included the name of a Center Street store. With this evidence, the agents could search for Russell and bring him to the police station.

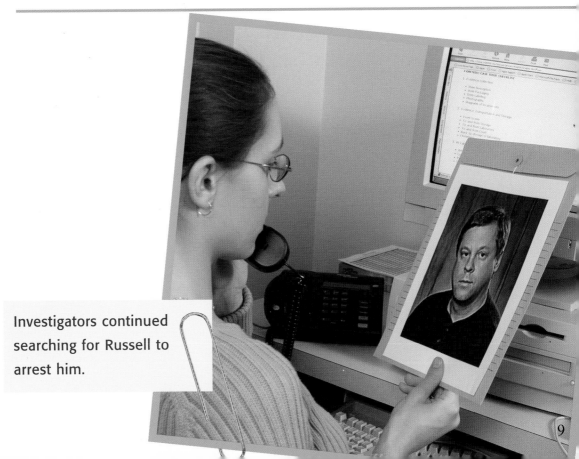

Investigators continued searching for Russell to arrest him.

CHAPTER 2

Learn about:

- Hackers
- The Phonemasters
- The Melissa virus

Types of Computer Crime

Since the early 1990s, the number of computer crimes has increased. Just one computer crime can affect computers all over the world.

Computer Crimes

People commit different types of computer crimes. They sometimes use computers to steal money. They also can find private information about other people. They may use this information to threaten others.

People who look for ways to break into computer systems are called hackers. Companies sometimes hire hackers to find weaknesses in their computer programs. Some hackers commit crimes by breaking into computer systems illegally.

◀ Hackers are skilled at finding information on computers.

David L. Smith pleaded guilty to creating the Melissa virus.

Some hackers break into phone companies' computers. This activity is called phreaking. During the early 1990s, a group of hackers called the Phonemasters learned the numbers of several calling cards. The cards were from AT&T, Sprint, and other large telephone companies. The Phonemasters used the numbers to make their own phone calls. Before the FBI arrested them, the phone companies had lost about $1 million.

Viruses

People sometimes send viruses into computer systems. A virus is a damaging computer program attached to another program or document. The virus starts after the program or document is opened. Viruses can make copies of themselves and affect other computers.

In 1999, the Melissa virus forced several large U.S. companies to shut down their e-mail systems. The virus began working when someone opened an infected e-mail. The virus then sent 50 e-mails to addresses in that computer's e-mail lists. Computer programmer David L. Smith pleaded guilty to creating the Melissa virus.

Robert Morris created a worm that caused thousands of computers to crash.

Worms

A worm is a damaging computer program similar to a virus. It hides inside a computer's hard drive. The worm makes copies of itself. It spreads to other computers through computer networks. Worms often cause computers to stop working, or crash.

In 1988, Robert Morris created the first worm that affected computers through the Internet. The worm caused thousands of U.S. computers to crash.

In 2003, FBI agents in Minneapolis, Minnesota, arrested teenager Jeffrey Lee Parson. He was arrested for sending a worm into the Internet. This worm was a form of an existing worm called the Blaster. But it was more damaging to computers. The worm infected about 7,000 personal computers across the United States. The infected computers kept starting up and shutting down.

Jeffrey Lee Parson was charged with creating a form of the Blaster worm.

CHAPTER 3

Learn about:
- Seizing computers
- Copying hard drives
- Finding fingerprints

Searching for Evidence

Investigators gather information about people they believe may have committed computer crimes. After investigators have a suspect, they may ask a judge for a search warrant. With a warrant, investigators can examine a suspect's computer.

Previewing and Seizing a Computer

Investigators often connect a laptop computer to a suspect's computer. The connection allows investigators to quickly peek at the computer's contents. If information relating to the case is found, investigators can seize the computer. A seized computer is taken away so it can be further examined.

Investigators can seize computers that
◀ contain information about a crime.

Investigators take photographs to keep track of their activities.

Investigators carefully handle a suspect's computer. They put on latex gloves before handling the computer. The gloves help protect any fingerprints that may be on the computer. Investigators often place the computer inside large paper bags. The bags protect fingerprints and other evidence.

Investigators keep a record of their activities. A record can be important if investigators need to talk about evidence in court. To keep a record, investigators take photographs as they work. They take photos of the computer and other equipment. They also take photos of the surrounding area. Some investigators record their activities with a video camera. The video gives investigators a detailed record of their work.

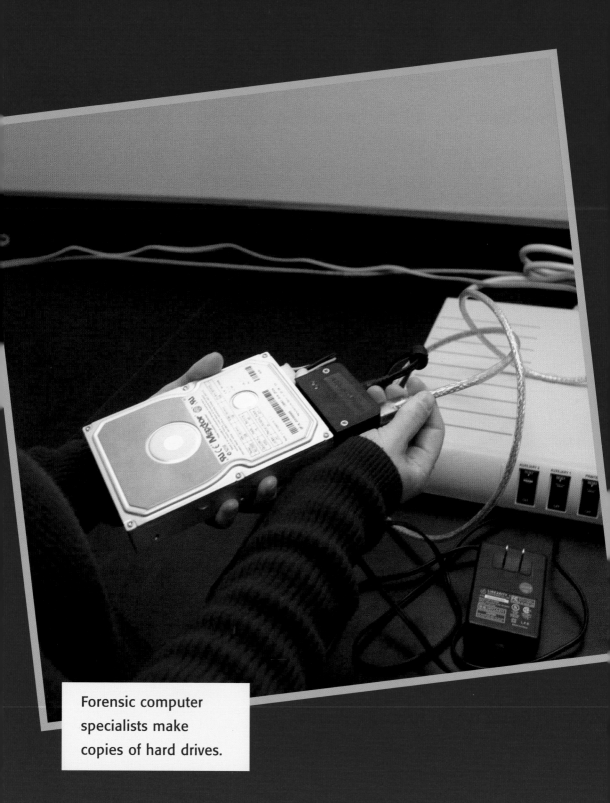

Forensic computer specialists make copies of hard drives.

Examining Hard Drive Copies

In a computer lab, forensic computer specialists examine computers. They take out a computer's hard drive. Much of a computer's information is stored on the hard drive.

Computer specialists make copies of the hard drive. They use software programs to examine the copies. Some programs find deleted or hidden files. Password-cracking programs help examiners find passwords. Text-searching programs allow examiners to search for certain words.

Sometimes computer forensic specialists can't view all information. Some information is private. Private information includes medical and legal records. Some warrants allow examiners to search for only certain types of evidence.

Hidden Bugs

Investigators sometimes place a tracking device called a bug inside a keyboard. They then return the suspect's computer. The device records each keystroke. Investigators can find out what was typed into the computer when they take out the bug.

A wireless recorder is another type of bug. The recorder sends the information being typed to an investigator's computer. Investigators can read a suspect's documents as they are being typed.

Searching for Fingerprints

Investigators examine a suspect's computer keyboard for fingerprints. Each person has different fingerprint patterns. Fingerprints can show who used the keyboard.

Investigators usually use lasers and other strong light sources to find fingerprints. The lights help investigators see the fingerprints without damaging the keyboard.

Investigators also can heat superglue to see fingerprints. Heated superglue gives off fumes that make prints visible.

Computer Terms

crash—to stop working

fry—to fail

glitch—an interruption in work or electric power

phreak—to hack into a phone network

ping—to send a message through a computer network checking for the presence of another computer or user

shoulder surf—to peek over a computer user's shoulder to gain secret information

sneaker—a person hired by a company to break into its security system to test it

spam—a large number of unwanted e-mails

CHAPTER 4

Fighting Computer Crime

Until the 1990s, law enforcement agencies had little equipment to help them fight computer crime. Today, several companies make programs for investigators. Many investigators also have training in computer forensics.

Computer Experts

The FBI and some state law enforcement agencies have computer experts. These experts can track computer worms and viruses. Sometimes they track computer information as it travels through thousands of miles of phone lines. They can track the route of a worm or virus until they find the original sender.

Investigators often use computers to help
◄ them find evidence.

Many of today's investigators take classes to learn how to handle computer crimes.

Investigators sometimes join computer clubs. They spy on club members to find out if illegal activities are happening. In 1990, the U.S. Secret Service investigated a group called the Legion of Doom. Some Secret Service agents joined the club to spy on its members. Police raided a Texas computer game company where one of the club members worked. The police seized much of the company's equipment as evidence.

Computer Labs

Workers at FBI labs examine digital evidence. Digital evidence can include information from personal computers, laptop computers, cell phones, or digital cameras.

In 2002, the FBI opened a computer lab in Menlo Park, California. FBI computer labs also are in Chicago, Kansas City, Dallas, and San Diego.

Damage from the 1993 World Trade Center bombing

A Terrorist Arrest

In 1995, police in the Philippines were spying on Abdul Hakim Murad. They believed he may have tried to kill Pope John Paul II. The police searched Murad's apartment. They found a laptop computer left behind by Ramzi Yousef. A forensic computer specialist examined the laptop computer. Documents in the computer linked Yousef to the 1993 World Trade Center bombing. Police arrested Yousef in Pakistan.

Computer evidence
can help investigators
solve cases.

Protecting Computers

Many computers have systems to prevent break-ins. Some programs block out viruses. Other programs protect passwords.

Some computers have a firewall. A firewall keeps track of information traveling from a network into a computer. People can set up a firewall to block out certain information.

Using Computer Evidence

Investigators sometimes use computer evidence in court. In 2003, investigators used a seized computer in the trial of John Allen Muhammad. Muhammad was found guilty of shooting people in the Washington, D.C., area.

Computer forensics is the fastest growing part of law enforcement. Security systems cannot protect computers from all break-ins. Investigators will continue working to solve even the newest computer crimes.

Glossary

e-mail (EE-mayl)—electronic messages that are sent between computers

fumes (FYOOMS)—gases, vapors, or smoke given off by chemicals

hacker (HAK-ur)—a person who looks for ways to break into computer systems

hard drive (HARD DRIVE)—a computer part that stores most of the computer's data

search warrant (SURCH WOR-uhnt)—an official piece of paper that gives permission to search a place for evidence

suspect (SUHSS-pekt)—someone thought to be responsible for a crime

Read More

DeAngelis, Gina. *Cyber Crimes.* Crime, Justice, and Punishment. Philadelphia: Chelsea House, 2000.

Grant-Adamson, Andrew. *Cyber Crime.* Crime and Detection. Broomall, Penn.: Mason Crest, 2003.

Judson, Karen. *Computer Crime: Phreaks, Spies, and Salami Slicers.* Issues in Focus. Berkeley Heights, N.J.: Enslow, 2000.

McIntosh, Neil. *Cyber Crime.* Face the Facts. Chicago: Raintree, 2003.

Internet Sites

FactHound offers a safe, fun way to find Internet sites related to this book. All of the sites on FactHound have been researched by our staff.

Here's how:

1. Visit *www.facthound.com*
2. Type in this special code **073682698X** for age-appropriate sites. Or enter a search word related to this book for a more general search.
3. Click on the **Fetch It** button.

FactHound will fetch the best sites for you!

Index